# REFLECTIONS
## *Past, Present and Future*

By Tana Brown

Order this book online at www.trafford.com
or email orders@trafford.com

Most Trafford titles are also available at major online book retailers.

Note for Librarians: A cataloguing record for this book is available from Library
and Archives Canada at www.collectionscanada.ca/amicus/index-e.html

Printed in Victoria, BC, Canada.

ISBN: 978-1-4269-1636-6 (sc)

*Our mission is to efficiently provide the world's finest, most comprehensive book publishing
service, enabling every author to experience success. To find out how to publish your book, your
way, and have it available worldwide, visit us online at www.trafford.com*

*Trafford rev. 9/3/2009*

 www.trafford.com

**North America & international**
toll-free: 1 888 232 4444 (USA & Canada)
phone: 250 383 6864 ♦ fax: 812 355 4082

# SPECIAL GRANDMOTHERS

People often speak of mothers and the unique thing they do
Yet, I never heard anyone praise you
They truly forgot all that you've done
And the many hearts you've won

How you took the time to explain
That life is not an easy game
Why god knew you could do the job
Of making life simple when it was hard

Often I wish to grow like you
For no one else in the world would do
That's why I'm taking this time to say
Grandma's are special every single day

They help ease the pain when you're blue
Never thinking twice as what to do
Therefore may your heart be forever my cover
As I will always be grateful to my grandmother

# DAD R.I.P

Oh heavenly father up above
Has taken away someone we love
It happen suddenly in the middle of the night
And he left without putting up a fight

Dad you left us here with pain and sorrow
Yet god not only had his eye on the sparrow
The lord said you needed a rest
And in our eyes he knows best

The times we had were all so great
And life with you wasn't a mistake
We thank god for our time together
Cause life with you couldn't have been better

You left a gift that we only can share
Although, we pray that god leads you back here
Our hearts are closed in your heavenly name
As our lives will never be the same

God has blessed us with you
This is something only he could do
Although you left we can't complain
Rest in peace dad in his heavenly name

## "EVERY"

Every time
Every thing
Wrong
Every word
Every feeling
Wrong
Every emotion
Every love
Wrong
Every time I try
Every thing I do
Every word I say
Every emotion I feel
Every love I have
Every touch I give
Every meaning I seek
All wrong
Every thing, time, word, emotion, love, touch meaning
All wrong
Now I search for right

# I'LL SEE YOU THEN

When your life is almost full
And you have accomplished
All you thought that you could
I'll see you then

That's because life has just begun
All those accomplishments
Are just treasured medals
Like what our soldiers have won

I'll see you then
Although you will have to be
At the right point in life
Just to reach me

And if I seem to fail
You can bet I'll try again
And just remember this
I will see you then

# HAPPY MOTHER'S DAY
## DAUGHTERS
## 2002

Magnificent you all may be
Outstanding to a mother like me
Trustworthy, which so  few are
Heart warming are my little stars
Extraordinary I'm happy to say
Ridiculously funny every minute of the day

Sometimes I have to admit these angels I must never forget
Distinguish are these ladies I adore
Astonishing and so much more
Yet I have to say
May you enjoy this mother's day

# DEAR LORD

Bless me, I am sad
Cause you want to take
The best grandma I have
I know you care as much as I do
But you should be aware of
How much I love her too

Dear Lord
Bless me, I may cry
Cause my grandma is about to die
I prayed to keep her here with me
But you said its time that she is free

Dear Lord
Thank you for the times we shared
Although it hurts more to loose someone
Who cares,
take her body and let her rest
just remember, dear lord
We loved her best

# "JAILED AGAIN"

Bow your head my son
But always stand tall
And you shall see my son
It's the white man that fall

Never forget the touch of life
And the woman that you love
Cause you can rest assure
She's worth thinking of

Let them be the boss
And always in command
Yet they shall all remember
You are the man

Spend time away and see
You must do as they say
And unfortunately my son
You pray when they say pray

But with yesterday gone
Tomorrow is here forever
And being the best of all
Makes you that much more cleaver

# I DREAM

It isn't about life and it's mysterious way
Cause I might not be allowed to see those glorious days
And if yesterday could be replayed again
Then tomorrow shall be my friend

It isn't about freedom nor slavery
For this is the life they gave me
And if last month would reappear
Then it's my life I'll cherish  so dear

It isn't about the living or the dead
Surely god wouldn't mess with my head
And if love would just give me a chance
It is then that I shall enhance

But for right know I dream
About life and what it really means
Now for today I'll wait and see
If in this world I'll ever be free!

# LIL LONELY GIRL

I hear the whispers from the ocean
As I listen to the cries of the sea
And I'm just wondering right now
If anyone cares about me

I often sit with head in hands
Along with a river of tears in my eyes
Yet no one answers my questions
Or even hear my cries

My only friends are pain and sorrow
While happiness just passes through
I wait for the time to come
When all my friends are new

I hide with the darkness of the night
I can't smile cause the pain is to severe
and any sound of laughter
Makes me run with fear

Lil Lonely girl be ready for
Bright days shall come real soon
And you'll see the sun set
As well as the rise of the moon

# YOU SAID I DO!!

The moment of truth has arrived
And you are no longer a bachelor
She is now your bride

He promised to love you
No matter what type of pain
He has taken the oath
And give you his name

You will always remember
Till death do us part
And her love will soon become
An important part of your heart

Forget about life's downfall
Focus on all the loving
Because you have a gift from god
A very distinguish husband

Love is the best medicine
In any ones life, and
This you do understand
Because you now have a wife

May your lives together be long lived
Just like a vintage of fine wine
Your love will always be tasteful
Because it shall enhance along with time

# THANK GOD FOR YOU

This isn't a note of despair
Just a little something I wrote
To show you a little more of how I care

I want to thank God for you
And all the precious things you do
Like showing how much you care
More so, just for being there

No my darling this isn't a note to frown
Its only to let you know that
I'm so damn glad you're around

God said he would always take care
And he did, by giving us our lives to share
He knew exactly how important it would be
So he sent you especially down to me

You're an angel, and guess what
No other angel would do
And that is why I thank God for you!

# OUR HEARTS, CRY

Use the powers of the heart
To get you through these times
And with a little help from god
All things would be fine

Open up your mind and soul
And see all that you can achieve
Look inside yourself my son
As the miracles you won't believe

Don't bow down to destruction
It will only lead you astray
Walk a straight line son
And be here for another day

No matter how hard it gets
I will always be there
Because you gave me a gift
That only a grandmother can share

# MOTHER

May every dream your dreaming,
Every hope and plan come true
May happiness surround you
And everything that you do

May this birthday be a start
Of a future that will bring
Many more happy birthdays
With the best of everything

So this comes from all of us
Those close and also far
We love you so much mother
Just the way you are

And with all those unique talents
We also wish to say
That no matter what tomorrow brings
Our love increase with each day

# GOLD

Gold was made for me
And I'll never give it away
I'll grow a diamond tree
And clean it every day

With fur in my closet
And silk on my bed
Like water from a faucet
I have nothing to dread

Now by the time my luck runs out
I'll be sitting in a cloud
And without any doubt
I am definitely very proud

Someday I'll even own a lake
Where the fish will go down stream
But soon I will awake
To find it's all a dream

# BOO–BEE

Who gave you the life you have today
No one else could have in a much kinder way
Where did you learn to be so polite
Think hard with all your might

Whose smile do you carry with grace
And bright eyes upon your face
Who said hold you head up very high
And forgave your mischief without a why

Now who was there to take away the pain
Come on I'm sure you remember the name
Who was by your side when you were sick
I'm sure that name you didn't forget

Run little girl and live not in fear
For your mother will always be there
Become a woman who wanted this
Your mother it was her only wish

# NEVER ME NEVER YOU

Remember the days when we were
Growing up it was never
Me or never you
It was always us

We did the job we broke
The lamp we said we'll never
Go away to boring camp

I cry, you cry, and I smiled
As you laughed how come
Those times are
The ones that have to pass

I ran away and you
Wanted desperately to come
My sister being alone
Is never going to be fun

Remember the time when we
Thought about what if we never
Came to be then it wouldn't
Have ever been you or never me

# PEANUT

Spoiled and rotten to the core
That's what you are and more
Gifted and wise is what I see
And that's how you appear to me

Special in your own little way
Loving and caring day-by-day
Giving all you can give
While trying your best just to live

Seeing the danger in your path
As hurt and pain just seem to last
But you've found time to pray
And with the lord is where you'll stay

Believe in yourself until the bitter end
Choose a dear and true friend
Let your mistakes teach you to learn
And then my love you would have truly earned

# CRYSTAL
# CONGRADULATIONS

Make this one of your
Happiest days my dear
For you will always remember
Your junior high school year

They will be filled with joy
Pain and sorrow too
But it will ease when
They think of you

You'll remember the laughter
And never understand the tears
But you will never ever
Forget your junior high school years

Thank that mean teacher
You know the one that didn't care
Thank her for the many times
She thought you wouldn't
go no where

Let them all know just
What you can really share
And how your life was spent
In your junior high school year

# LOST MY BABY

I'm very lonely and almost always sad
Cause I lost the only love I ever had
Just like you loose your money
I done lost my honey

Yes it was by mistake I need him so
But god knows he had to go
Even though I'll never understand why
I found it very hard to say goodbye

It's like giving up your favorite pair of jeans
He can turn fantasies into dreams
Stop a tear before it can fall
And say so much in a ten minute call

He makes you love him all so much
As he seduces you without even a touch
Sets your soul on more than just fire
Amazingly quenches your every desire

But my baby just ran out of luck
He may have even spent his last buck
Cause I'm not there you see
Now I wonder if my baby still loves me

# BLIND

As I wake I see a face
One that isn't so very clear
Then I wonder through the day
Is this the father I lost last year

I can't hear the words often spoken
Or feel a touch as I hold a hand
Missing his smile is just as bad
But I can't find him throughout this land

I've tried so hard to reach out to him
Although I have yet to feel his touch
And I know I'll keep trying to reach him
Cause I miss him all so much

Don't matter though cause I'll see him soon
Then it's back to visits and sleeping in his room
But for now I'll just toss and turn
Cause my daddy's dead this I have to learn

# WHITE AND BLACK

Darkie, darkie move this way
On this line is where niggers pray
Don't be upset by what I've just said
Cause you are a nigger or your dead

You can name us whatever you wish
You can serve our pride out on a dish
But we have what all white people need
Which is love, and it's pure breed

Lil girl don't walk through that door
You'll leave your black footprint on the floor
Go around and enter from the back
Because niggers aren't welcome here and that's a fact

We have understanding love and much more
And that's what we wish to leave at your door
Our color we know cause we can see
But we are no longer niggers we are free

# YES MY FATHER

Who can work all day
With little pay
Yes my father

Who can love all night
Without putting up a fight
Yes my father

Who cares in every little way
And still to the lord he pray
Yes my father

And now who have left us all alone
As we sit around his body to moan
Yes my father

But who have left us all so much
That only our hearts can now touch
Yes my father

# FRIENDSHIP

Friendship is something that you earn
And being your friend this I've learned
But as far as I can see
I've lost my friendship over a fantasy

You've taught me ways to express myself clear
Showed me how life could  be lived without fear
Knowing the price I would have to pay
I went and gambled our friendship away

Let me see if I could patch things up
And show you why your friendship means so much
Friends come only once in a blue moon
And I know another will not come to soon

Friendship is hard to come by
And the thought of loosing yours make me cry
Tears that can be turned into joy
The moment your friendship walks back threw the door

# STRANGERS THAT WE ARE

STRANGERS THAT WE ARE
VERY NEAR IN OUR MIND
HOPE THIS IS THE ONE
LOVE IS WHAT I WANT TO FIND

IT SHALL HAPPEN BEFORE I KNOW
MY HEART WILL SKIP A BEAT
I WON'T BE ABLE TO EXPLAIN
WHY LOVE I CAN'T DEFEAT

STRANGERS THAT WE ARE
FAR AWAY IN SIGHT
STILL HOPING YOU'RE THE ONE
THAT WILL GET MY HEART SOARING IN FLIGHT

FOR NOW I'LL JUST WONDER
WHAT LOVE WILL BE LIKE
AND WHEN I MEET IT
WILL IT SHINE LONG AND BRIGHT

# OUR WEDDING POEM
## JULY 19, 2003

Congratulations is in order
For this day you've set aside
He has become your husband
And you are now his bride

## MAE

Many would come to say
What a very special time
But you are so unique mommy
As we know, what's on your mind

## MAC

Very few has touched her heart
And all of ours above
Yet you have become the father
That we truly, truly love

We now give you this gift
Wrapped with more than just care
Which is our endless love
For the both of you to share

# MY GODMOTHER
# VIRGINIA

You showed me that godmothers are great
By all the laughter you gave to me
I otherwise might not have seen
That life is better with we

You helped spring me
Into the woman I am today
And no matter how hard the task
You never forget to pray

You loved me no matter what
Even when I wasn't around
I'm glad you didn't give up
For my love you have found

So godmother I love you
From the bottom of my heart
As this is only the beginning
And the loving shall never stop

# JAIL

Not enough love in your life
Just a lot of regrets and pain
So powerful it can make
You forget your given name

Out of shame and guilt
Between pity surrounded by sorrow
You wonder with a sign of relief
What if this life is only borrowed

Too much violence for your eyes to see
Where life comes and goes all in a day
And at the ripe old age of five
You say "when do I get to play"

Strange as your life maybe
I must say this is honestly true
No matter what the reason
I found a son in you

Son, I haven't much experience with boys
Nor do I have the answer to every problem
But together my loving son I know
That will definitely solve them

Be ready to go through the extreme
Never again shall you require bail
As I know for sure my son
You shall never be in jail

# HOW WE MET

I wasn't scared
When you entered the room
But I didn't know
Our love will enhance soon

I wasn't nervous
Yet my hand tremble with fear
And I may never admit
How my heart pound when you were near

I wasn't being sneaky
Although I didn't want you to see
Just how much I blushed
When you came next to me

I now must be honest
Cause my heart would show
Just how much I love you
And now the world has to know

# I'M HERE, AM I

Just beyond yesterday
One flight below time
And I hope for the impossible
Is this life truly mine

I have to struggle
To get on the right track
And the pain is overwhelming
For now I'm the token black

The guide my life needed
Was spike with betray
And what then followed
My life was put on display

A story not to be real
In which experience is just a fake
And the reality of my life
Someone shall soon take

# DADDY

I know we haven't been in touch
But I miss you all so much
As my world come falling apart
You are always there in my heart

You leaving left a gap in my mind
And only your love can replace it this time
Something I know you'll never complete
Until in heaven when again we meet

All the tears I shed are so painfully true
Cause I sadly miss the love from you
As the days pass and time goes by
I sit and wonder but often I cry

I hope to visit before I come to an end
And express how your more than dad but a friend
Thank you for all that you gave
And it's your love that I have save

# I MUST NEVER FORGET

Sorry to have forgotten
The day we came to be
But I am never sorry
That you shared your love with me

It's the best anyone could want
From the beginning to the very end
It shows you all types of respect
And the true meaning of a friend

All the blows from the wind
All the winters white storms
Make me realize that
Loving you was never wrong

Every time the rain falls
Or a tear start to drop
I think of your love
And the pain seems to stop

Thank you for the life we shared
As I hope it would never end
Although I wouldn't get mad
If we tried to do it again

So when I'm feeling blue
And my emotions are falling apart
I will always love you
From the bottom of my heart

# THE JEWS OF SADDLE BROOK

Sorry or forgiveness isn't right due
But that's what I send to all of you
With sadness and pity at the very top
While your beliefs should never have to stop

As reality out do unbearable pain
Only then will you feel truly sane
And send out your message of belief
That prejudices your soon shall defeat

It has to stop so you can mend
All the ungrateful times you've been in
Allowing all to heal and not be ashamed
Of life and your given name

Be brave hold on and try to understand
That those people are only a fraction of man
Jews also value the beauty of a pearl
And they to should have a part of this world

Crying out for revenge just don't define
Why the evil always out do the kind
And if you can, what shall you change
Definitely not the value of your name

To the Jews of unfortunate crime
This all shall heal with a matter of time
But since I see you can't seem to bare
This is someone who honestly cares

So in your hours of disbelief
I to share your pain and grief
And I know that we shall overcome
What this ungrateful world has done

To the Jews of saddle brook
From a mother of three, who wants to be free

# THROUGH MY EYES

My heavenly father up above
Has taken away someone I love
So lift my spirits up so very high
As I try to understand why

I thought a dream is a path to the future
And ensuring quite belief of the heart
And just like my love ones
I wish them to never depart

My heavenly father please confirm
That this lesson I haven't earned
I didn't tell any forbidden lie
Nor did I ask for anyone to die

Now I know you may feel abandon
As your heart is all so shallow
Just remember that god
Not only has his eyes on the sparrow

My heavenly father so wise and true
Surely knows what I'm going through
But dear god be extra special to him
Because he was more than just a friend

# WHY I CRY
## 2-24-04

Only when I can't see you
The water comes to eye
And that's one reason
Why I cry

Like the time you came over
Then left without a goodbye
Made me realize again
Why I cry

When your hugs are few
I truly can't deny
At that point in my life is
Why I cry

Everytime I say I love You
And never get a reply
That's when I remember
How much I cry

# I'M COMING HOME

I SAW IN YOUR EYES
A MOMENT OF DISPEAR
AT THAT TIME I KNEW
THAT YOU DO MORE THAN CARE

YOU ALLOWED THE SUN TO RISE
SHOWED ME THE BEAUTY IN THE MOON
AND ENLIGHTEN ME WITH EVERY CLOUD PASSING BY
BABY I'M COMING HOME REAL SOON

I FELT THE TEAR YET
YOU NEVER LET IT FALL
I HEAR THE SADNESS IN YOUR VOICE
WITH EACH AND EVERY CALL

I'M COMING HOME YOU'LL SEE
AND I'LL EASE YOUR TROUBLE HEART
TAKE AWAY ALL THE PAIN
BECAUSE IT'S TILL DEATH DO US PART

# "YES I LIVE"

I live with pain
While playing with sorrow
Took a chance on
Seeing a new tomorrow

Heartache is a friend
And freedom just a word
Not knowing who I am
Is a life I don't deserve

Can't wait to meet pride
Joy is welcome here too
And if love should pass by
I wouldn't know what to do

Right now I'll just pray
Hope and wish also
That when love do hit
More than just my heart will know

# I CAN'T SAY

I CAN'T SAY I DON'T LOVE YOU
BECAUSE THAT WOULD BE A LIE
I CAN'T SAY I MISS YOU
CAUSE THAT WOULD MAKE YOU CRY

I TRIED MANY NIGHTS
TO SAY THESE WORDS TO YOU
YET THEY HAVEN'T EMERGED
ALTHOUGH MY LOVE IS TRUE

CLOSEST TO MY HEART
IS WHERE YOU BELONG
AND LOVING YOU LIKE I DO
SURELY CAN'T BE WRONG

SO AS HIGH AS THE MOUNTAINS
AND AS DEEP AS THE SEA
I BELONG TO YOU AND
YES YOU BELONG TO ME

# HOW ABOUT A SHORT POEM

Without reason you came
No special occasion was near
Yet the gift you gave
Made my life more clear

Every sound you make
Each moan and groan
Makes me come to the thought
That my heart isn't alone

The passion that engulfs my world
Is truly heaven sent
And without your heart
It wouldn't be worth a cent

Thank you my darling
For not playing a game
As I truly do love you
And I'm not ashame

# "NOW I PRAY"

Oh heavenly father I beg of you
Help change my life around
Before it's to late
No more pain and sorrow
I've had all I can take

I've made some mistakes,
Done some ungodly things
Took life for granted
Because I didn't know what it means

Now I bow my head down
With shame and disgust
Although god will forgive me
First I must earn his trust

Deliver me from this unworthy life
Please light the way to your heart
I would like to understand your will
Before my world unwillingly depart

# GOING AWAY

I can't come to ends
With reality and me
I have no understanding
Yet I wish to be free

I found just how to love
Now I know what it means
Just can't believe that
Reality is more than a dream

I could never make a promise
Although I wish to comply
With all life offering
But they just seem to be a lie

Now you know about me
And the reason for the betray
Therefore you will understand
Why I just can't stay

# GOD KNEW

Yes God did hear
He listened to my cries
And decided it was my turn
To dry up my eyes

Yes god didn't understand
Why my world was in a uproar
Or why my pain was so severe
So he knew I couldn't take no more

Yes god did agree
That my life wasn't mine
He knew I needed a lift
And it now was my time

I would never have to worry
That I'll ever be alone
Because you are now my world
With a love I can call my own

# I REMEMBER

I remember the first time
When we embraced in a kiss
I felt my life was complete
With all that I've missed

I recall the first touch
The one that made me say
I wish this could be forever
Returning day by day

I imagine the respect
The chance I got to reply
Just the way I feel
And it wouldn't be a lie

Now I'm in love
With someone who cares
Although I may never understand
But my love I get to share

# MY LIFE

Time is passing at a strange rate
As I try to collect and conserve
Regardless of what I've learned
My life has yet to emerge

I have questions of reasons
But often given answers of lies
And just like the old oak tree
I wait hopelessly to die

I'm still so very puzzled
About life and it's doors
And I'm honestly wondering
What if my life was truly yours

I try to accomplish many things
Although I still don't know
That what life has to offer
Doesn't come on a television show

Now with all that trying
And wishing to be free
I shall have my own rewards
But first I must know me

# FAREWELL FRIEND

How many times did you
Call my name and say
Have more confidence
And you'll master the day

How about these words of wisdom
Unavailable too high and supervisor approve
Well, watch these too and
I'm sure you'll rule

I want to thank you
For the tough things taught
For believing in me
When I got hooked and caught

May your new family
Treat you with respect
Most important Lucrecia
May this family you never
Forget

# IF

If I could only believe
That you wanted to go
Will set my heart at ease
And the tears will no longer flow

If I could only understand
That you lived your life here
And we place you in gods hands
As your heart will Forever be near

If I could only pray
It wouldn't be very hard
Because you lived the right way
And is accepted by god

If this is really the end
And you have moved on
My heart wouldn't be grieving
And you wouldn't be gone

If I could only believe
That This is for the best
And god knows what he is doing
Then mother please do rest

# I CRIED

You reminded in every call
That tomorrow you might not be here
I didn't want to believe it
So I would close my ears

I never wanted you to be free
Although I prayed to end you sorrow
I even asked god for once to
Remove his eye from that sparrow

I'm sorry for the tears
I know you said don't cry
But some how big brother
I never expected you to die

My world is now scorn
And this is tearing me apart
Yet always remember Reggie
You'll have a permanent place
In my heart

# CALL ME

When your life doesn't
Feel like your own precious stones
Call me and I'll mend
All your weary bones

If you can't smile
And life just puts you down
Call me so I can
Lift you from the ground

As you try to hold you head high
And walk with no shame
Call me as I know how
To shift all the blame

Now that you are sure
Your life is worth living
Call me because
It's my love I'll be given

When, if, as and now
Are the words often spoken
Call me and my heart
Will be just a small token

# I'M WONDERING

I am wondering
What makes me happy
Then I though of you

I often remembered
What puts a smile on my face
All of sudden I knew

My world has become
An enchanted life of love
What a magical place to be

I will never forget
The sorrow in my life
Or the problems that haunted me

I know I love you
With more than a pure heart
And it's tainted with gods wishes too

I am now feeling blessed
Honored to stand by your side
And as nothing can replace my love for you!

# BYE -BYE DADDY

Life without my father
Has been a living hell
When ever I remember him
I get lost, entangled in a spell

Can't say I'll ever be the same
Wouldn't want anyone to hear
My cries of hurting
Cause my daddy isn't here

As I enjoy a sunny day
My heart starts to pound
And all my thoughts
Are of my daddy in the ground

He left me with thoughts
Of how he made me smile
The joy is what I remember
Being with him as a child

I love you more than you could imagine
Yet my heart was torn apart
Even though he left me
My loving never did stop

# NOT MY TURN

I grew up with pain
Never new anything but pity
Always wondered why I was alone
Living in a great big city

My best friend was shame
Sorrow lived down the street
And let me tell you this
Freedom I can't wait to meet

I had more wishes
As well as hope and dreams
Then anyone could have
I just want to understand what life
Really means

For now I'll continue to pray
And wait to my chance to flourish
That's the time I know
My life I will forever cherish

# "THE WILD"

Staking the night
Looking for a lead
Just want something
So that he could feed

Working to keep up with the lads
Hoping that no one would find
Any of the little mouth watering
Meals as he search another time

Teaching the way to hunt
And get a great meal
Sometime a little will do
Just until your next steal

The wildlife is really boring
You must hunt for your dinner
And there's no telling
If what you catch is a winner

# "SORRY TO SHOW"

Sorry to have displayed
So much affection
I'm so used to
Getting everyday rejection

Sorry to let you know
How I truly feel
Often I'm told
That love is for real

Sorry I have to said
I love you so much
Although you already know
You got the magic touch

Sorry that I've been
Always peeking at your feet
From morning, to noon and all night
Your loving is so sweet

I'm glad to show you
Just how much you mean to me
And that were going to spend
Our lives together till eternity

# GOD 2

GOD WHEN I WAKE I PRAY
THAT I MAKE IT THROUGH
NOT TOMORROW, BUT ONLY TODAY

GOD WHEN I SLEEP I DREAM
ABOUT REMOVING THESE DRUGS
OUT OF MY STREAM

YES GOD I TRULY WISH
THAT MY NAME BE ADDED
TO YOUR GOING HOME LIST

OH, YEAH GOD I NOW ACCLAIM
THAT USING AND ABUSING DRUGS
WASN'T A PART OF THE GAME

GOD IF I HAD JUST ONE LIFE TO LIVE
I THEN WOULD CHOOSE TO DIE
SO YOU CAN HAVE A BIGGER HEART
TO SPEAD ACROSS THE SKY.

# YOUR BEST FRIEND

I REMEMBER YOUR CALL
IT WAS ONE OF DISTRESS
TRYING TO TELL ME THAT
YOUR TIRED AND NEED TO REST

I NEVER UNDERSTOOD WHY
YOUR PAIN I COULDN'T SHARE
OR WHY YOUR LIFE
GOD COULDN'T SPARE

GOD HAS A NEW ANGEL
ONE IN WHICH I'VE MET
NOW HE'S THE LUCKY ONE
BECAUSE HE HAS THE BEST ONE YET

YOUR HOME AT LAST
AS YOUR TRAVELS HAVE NOW END
ETERNITY WITH THE LORD
OUR FATHER, YOUR NEW BEST FRIEND

# ONE

THE JOKE IS OVER
THE LAUGTHER IS DONE
YOU AND GOD HAVE
NOW BECOME AS ONE

YOU SHALL SMILE FOREVER
AND PAIN, WELL THERE'S NONE
YOU WILL WALK WITH GOD
NO YOU, NO HIM, ONLY ONE

ASHES TO ASHES I PRAY
WE KNOW THE TIME WILL COME
WHEN LIFE ON HEAVEN AND EARTH
WILL BE JOINED AS ONE

OPEN THE HEAVENLY GATES
AND WELCOME YOUR NEW SON
EMBRACE YOUR SOUL WITH GOD
BECAUSE YOU ARE NOW ONE

# I MISSED IT

I SAW THE SUN
HIGH UP IN THE SKY
BUT WHAT I DIDN'T CATCH
WAS YOUR LOVE PASSING BY

SOMEHOW IT WENT OVER MY HEAD
LIKE THE HOWLING OF THE WIND
I NEVER GOT THE CHANCE
TO INVITE YOUR LOVE IN

AS FAST AS THE STREAMS FLOW
WHILE STANDING NEXT TO THE HOLLOW TREE
THE LOVE I SHOULD HAVE GOTTEN
VANISHED INTO THE SEA

I WOULD HAVE CHASED IT DOWN
BUT THE TIDE WAS TO STRONG
SO NOW ALL I CAN DO
IS WAIT, I HOPE NOT FOR LONG

YES I WILL GET A SECOND CHANCE
TO SHOW YOU HOW I FEEL
AND YOU WILL SURELY SEE
THAT MY LOVE IS FOR REAL

# REGGIE

REGGIE I HAVEN'T BEEN TO SEE YOU
AND I MISSED YOUR CARD THIS YEAR
REGGIE I REALLY LOVE YOU
AND YOUR VOICE I WISH TO HEAR

REGGIE I'VE BEEN DOWN AND OUT
I DON'T HAVE THE SHOULDER I NEED
AND NOBODY UNDERSTANDS ME
REGGIE THIS YOU MUST BELIEVE

REGGIE I'M STILL CRYING
AND A WHOLE YEAR WENT BY
REGGIE LIFE IS SO SHABBY CAUSE
YOUR NOT HERE TO KEEP MY EYES DRY

REGGIE THIS COMES FROM MY HEART
MAY WE SEE EACH OTHER IN HEAVEN
SO THE PAIN COULD SUBSIDE
YOUR LAUGTHER IS WHAT I CRAVE

# THE PATH

HE LAID DOWN A WAY
FOR US TO GO TOWARDS
HE ALSO LET US KNOW
THAT HIS LIFE IS TRULY YOURS

HIS HEART IS AN OPEN BOOK
TO THOSE WHO ARE TRUE
HE INVITES THE LESS FORTUNE
TO HAVE A LIFE A NEW

JUST WONDER ABOUT JESUS
AND WHAT HE REALLY MEANS
LOOK AROUND YOUR WORLD
AS REALITY REPLACES ALL DREAMS

YES GOD IS WITH YOU
AND HE IS NOT ASHAME
JUST PUT YOUR BEST FOOT FORWARD
AND YOU'LL NEVER FORGET HIS NAME

# LOVE

THEY SAY LOVE, AND HAPPINESS
YET THEY NEVER REALLY KNEW
THAT I WAS HOOKED ON
ALCOHOL AND DRUGS TOO

NOT MANY PEOPLE WOULD UNDERSTAND
WHAT LIFE WITHOUT LOVE IS LIKE
IT'S THE EARTH MOVING FROM HEAVEN
OR WAKING UP WITHOUT ANY SITE

TOO MANY TIMES I PRAY FOR
A GOOD SOLID TREAT
INSTEAD ALL I EVER ENCOUNTER
IS DRUGS ON THE STREET

HEY MY TIME IS NOW
I AM HAPPY AS CAN BE
BECAUSE I GET LOVE FROM
GOD, AND IT'S FREE

# RESPECT

CAUGHT UP IN DISPEAR
AS I TRY TO RECOLLECT
WHY I HAVEN'T BEEN GETTING
ANY TYPE OF RESPECT

BY ALLOWING NATURE IN YOUR HEART
I'M SURE YOU WON'T REGRET
THE FEELING YOU GET FROM
HAVING A LITTLE BIT OF RESPECT

IN ORDER TO GET YOU MUST GIVE
NEVER LASHING OUT TO NEGLECT
LIVE YOU LIFE TO THE FULLEST
AND YOU WOULD HAVE EARNED YOUR RESPECT

LOOK UP HIGH ABOVE THE SKY
GO PASS THE CLOUDS WE OFTEN FORGET
THEN YOU CAN THANK GOD
FOR ALL THE LOVE AND RESPECT

# ANXIETY

I COULD HAVE LIVED
FREE OF ALL TYPES OF PAIN
INSTEAD I CHOOSE TO HAVE
ANXIETY DRIVE ME INSANE

JUST BECAUSE I COULDN'T SEE
WHAT REALLY WAS GOING ON
I LEFT THE DOORS OPEN
THAT'S WHEN ANXIETY CAME ALONG

IT HITCHED A RIDE
RIGHT IN THE MIDDLE OF MY HEART
AS LIFE WENT ON IT ALLOWED
DEPRESSION TO RIDE ON TOP

I COULDN'T SHAKE IT
BUT KNEW I HAD TO BREAK FREE
SO I PRAYED TO GOD
TO LIFT ANXIETY AND DEPRESSION OFF ME.

# GOD'S SLAVE

AMERICA WASN'T BUILT IN A DAY
NEITHER WAS OUR ADDICTION TO ALCOHOL
OUR EMONTIONAL STATE ALLOWED US
TO DRINK MORE THAN WE COULD AFFORD

WE TRY EVERYTIME TO JUSTIFY
WHY WE DRINK AND USE DRUGS
NEVER REALIZING ONE REASON COULD
BE THE LACKING OF GETTING HUGS

YES WE ARE IN DENIAL
AND IF THE TRUTH WAS HEARD
OUR EARDRUMS WOULD POP
AS WE STUMBLED OUT EACH WORD

AMERICA YOU USED EVERYTHING SO WE COULD GET
HIGH
AND YOU WERE OVER GENERIOUS IN WHAT YOU GAVE
SORRY YOU NO LONGER HOLD THE ROPE
WE ARE NOW GOD'S SLAVE

# GOD

GOD CAN YOU TELL ME
HOW MY WORLD SHOULD END
YOU HAVE JUST ALLOWED LIGHT
INTO A PLACE OFTEN DIM

GOD WOULD YOU EXPLAIN WHY
LIFE IS SO PAINFUL TO THE HEART
I NOW KNOW ONCE ISN'T ENOUGH
TO TEAR THIS WORLD APART

GOD I WANT TO UNDERSTAND
LIFE AND IT'S UNIQUE WAYS
LIKE THE TIME WHEN YOU
SHOWED ME HOW GOOD IT FEELS TO PRAY

GOD I KNOW MY LIFE IS ALL MY OWN
AND ALL THE GOOD AND BAD I DO
BUT JUST FOR ONCE IN THIS LIFE TIME
GOD I WANT TO BE LIKE YOU

# NAT

SOME PEOPLE SAY CRAZY THINGS
OTHERS DON'T SAY JACK
BUT WHATS SO DIFFERENT
IS MY FRIEND NAT

NAT IS TAN WITH AN A
YET EVERYONE ALREADY KNEW
AND IF YOU TURNED IT AROUND
IT BECOMES NAT THROUGH AND THROUGH

NAT MEANS LAUGTHER
A JOKE SO WELL TOLD
THAT IT'S STILL FUNNY
EVEN AFTER YOUR ONE HUNDERD YEARS OLD

KINDNESS IS ONE OF HIS TRAITS
AND HIS HEART IS MADE OF GOLD
IF YOU EVER GET THE CHANCE TO MET HIM
YOU'LL UNDERSTAND WHY HIS FRIENDSHIP I HOLD

# MY BATTLE

I TRIED FOR MANY YEARS
TO STAY CLEAN AND SOBER
KNOWING THAT ANOTHER DRINK
AND MY LIFE WOULD BE OVER

I WOULD HIT THE BOTTLE
WITH UNDESIRABLE BEHAVIOR
NOT CARING WHAT WOULD HAPPEN
JUST AS LONG AS LIQUOR WAS ON THE LABEL

MY REACTION WAS TO FIND
THE PERFECT SCAPEGOAT
SO NO ONE WOULD BELIEVE
I WAS STRUNG OUT ON DOPE

IN ANALYZING WHAT WENT WRONG
AND REALIZING THERE WAS NO ONE TO BLAME
I PRAYED TO MY HIGHER POWER
FREE ME IN HIS HEAVENLY NAME

# THE FIGHT

I FOUGHT THE BATTLE
OF THE MISUNDERSTOOD
I STOOD UP TO THE POWERFUL SHAME
ALTHOUGH I NEVER HAD A CHANCE
I STILL BEAT THE GAME

I'VE SWIMMED IN THE OCEAN
TOOK ON THE FISH IN THE SEA
NOW I KNOW WHAT IT'S MEANT
BY I JUST WANT TO BE FREE

ALTHOUGH THE FIGHT WASN'T FAIR
I CHALLANGED THE GREAT ONE
AND IF I COULD ONLY END
THIS BATTLE NO SOONER THAN DONE

THE REWARD WASN'T A WIN
THE OUTCOME WASN'T A PRETTY SITE
I'VE BATTLED WITH HELL
NOW IT'S THE DEVIL I MUST FIGHT

# KIONNA

YOU HAVE JUST EXPERIENCED
ONE OF LIFES FLAWS
YOU MAY EVEN BE WONDERING
IF THIS LIFE IS YOURS

IF YOU WALK WITH RESPECT
AND MAKE DIGNITY YOU BEST FRIEND
I KNOW THAT FOR SURE
YOUR HEART WILL MEND

FACE THIS WORLD WITH MORE
THAN JUST AN OPEN MIND
WHILE TRYING TO UNDERSTAND THE DIFFICULTY
I'M SURE YOU'LL BE FINE

IF LOVE WASN'T A WORD
AND PEACE IS ONE OF YOUR GOALS
YOU MUST NEVER FORGET
THAT IT'S MY HEART THAT YOU HOLD

# THE CHILDREN

SOME PEOPLE WISH FOR RICHES
OTHERS FOR THE PAIN TO GO AWAY
BUT MY WISH, DEAR LORD IS
TO MAKE MY KIDS SAFE

PROTECT THEM FROM  STRAY BULLET
LIKE THE ONE AIMING FOR THEIR HEAD
BECAUSE I KNOW FOR SURE LORD
LIFE WOULD BE HELL IF THEY WERE DEAD

LIFT  THERE SOULS BEYOND THE TREES
ALLOW THEM TO EMBRACE THE HEAVENS ABOVE
SO THEY WILL UNDERSTAND THAT
JUST LIKE ME, YOU TOO SHARE THEIR LOVE

THIS PRAY ISN'T FOR ME
OR JUST FOR THE CHILDREN THAT I BARE
BUT ALSO FOR THE LITTLE ONES
WHOSE VOICE YOU BARELY HEAR.

# SINCERELY, THE CALL

THIS ISN'T TO MAKE YOU SAD
AND IT SURELY DON'T WISH FOR YOU TO CRY
BUT GOD ONLY KNOWS WHY
IT WAS YOUR BROTHERS TURN TO DIE

IT WASN'T DONE OUT OF SPITE
NOTHING MEAN WAS INTENT
IT'S JUST THE LORD'S WAY OF SAYING
I CALLED AND HE WENT

THE SORROW WE FEEL SOMETIMES
WE WILL NEVER UNDERSTAND
YET HE'S OUT OF HARMS WAY
AND NOW IS IN GODS HANDS

THE LOVE YOU SHARED
SHALL FOREVER BE IN YOUR HEART
AND BELIEVE ME, NOT EVEN DEATH
COULD TEAR THAT APART

LET NOT THIS LOST
BE YOUR DOWN FALL
JUST BE READY MY FRIEND
WHEN GOD SENDS YOU HIS CALL

# BIG BROTHER

I WAS JUST WONDERING
WHO WOULD I TURN TO
WHEN MY LIFE IS IN AN UP ROAR
BEING THAT I NO LONGER HAVE YOU

WHEN I FEEL THE NEED
TO TALK ABOUT A FEELING
TELL ME WHO WOULD LISTEN
PLEASE LET ME KNOW WHO IS WILLING

AND SUPPOSE I WANT TO CRY
WHOSE SHOULDER COULD I LEAN ON
UNFORTUNELY NOT YOURS BIG BRO
BECAUSE YOUR NOT HERE, YOUR GONE


YET MEMORIES OF LAUGTHER
GIVEN TO ME FROM YOU
IS SOMETHING ONLY MY
BIG BROTHER CAN DO

# I ASKED GOD FOR HELP

Just before my last hit
I asked god to help me quit
Give me a sign to make me wonder
At that time I went under

Unable to grasp reality by the hand
As I struggled to keep balance and stand
I asked god just what to do
Right at that moment I knew I was through

Never understood how to cope
Where to get help was their hope
I knew the war was going to be hard
That's when I prayed to god

I needed assistance to end the obsession
Didn't think it would happen with only a confession
So I did it cold turkey
And I knew then god wouldn't hurt me

# SHOW ME

I am willing to give up
My destruction of drugs
And take my chances with
Gods way of being loved

I want to see pass the pain
Forget about the life I have done
Reach far beyond the stars
So I and Jesus can be one

I have a burning heart
Filled with regret and sin
Yet my soul has eternity
If only I'll give it to him

Let me not be afraid
Of what I don't understand
Show me the way to become
Like Jesus god's right hand man

# A PRINCESS LOST

As we grieve for such a lost
We've often filled with pain and sorrow
But, we must remember that god
Not only has his eyes on the sparrow

There must have been at least one time
When he has turned away to see
Just what unique type of gift
He has shined upon me

A charming irreplaceable Princess
Sophisticated as a woman should be
Straight from Buckingham palace she came
Motivated, compassionate, criticized yet free

I put these words together because
Being just plain old sorry won't do
Therefore Princess Diana meant to me
Just as much as she meant to you

The time has come to say good-bye
But this part of life I really can't do
So forever in my heart Princess Diana
Is where I place you

# DAWN A FRIEND

FRIENDS HAVE TO BE REAL
ALWAYS GIVEN A HONEST OPINION
KEEPING YOU FOREVER AT EASE
EVEN WHEN YOUR HEAD IS SPINNING

FRIENDS HAS TO BE UNQUIE
FOR THEY POSSESS A CERTAIN POWER
ONE THAT THEY SEEM TO USE
EVERY MINUTE OF THE HOUR

FRIENDS ARE ALWAYS THEIR
EVEN WHEN YOU DON'T WANT THEM TO
AND SOME HOW IF THEIR NOT
YOU WOULDN'T KNOW WHAT TO DO

FRIENDS ARE FOREVER
THEY CLING TO YOUR LOVING HEART
AND IF ANYTHING SHOULD HAPPEN TO THEM
IT WOULD SADLY TEAR YOU APART

A LITTLE REMINDER OF A FRIEND
AND JUST WHAT THEY CAN DO
NOW THE REAL REASON I'M SAYING THIS
IS DAWN I FOUND A FRIEND IN YOU

# MY GIFT TO YOU

THERE ARE MANY GIFTS
THAT YOU CAN HAVE
YET ONLY ONE WILL
SURELY MAKE YOU GLAD

NO FLOWERS OF BEAUTY
NOT EVEN A DIAMOND OR A PEARL
SHALL HAVE THE PROMISING EFFECT
OF THE LOVE FROM YOUR GIRL

NO THIS GIFT YOU CAN'T BUY
THERE ISN'T A PRICE TO PAY
AND THE CHERISHED MOMENT
WILL BE APART OF YOUR EVERYDAY

SO TAKE THIS GIFT TO HEART
SHARE IT WITH ONLY YOUR LOVE
THEN YOU WILL COME TO REALIZE
THIS GIFT IS FROM GOD ABOVE

# TIME AFTER TIME

YESTERDAY I LOOKED INTO YOUR EYES
TODAY I THOUGHT ABOUT WHAT I SAW
BELIEVE IT OR NOT MY LOVE
I WISHED I COULD SEE SOME MORE

THE CANDLES WERE BURNING BRIGHT
AS THE FIREPLACE CRACKLED WITH LOVE
MY HEART POUNDED WITH JOY
BECAUSE IT WAS ME YOU WERE THINKING OF

I NEVER WANTED TO TURN AWAY
AFRAID I WOULD MISS THE CHANCE
TO SEE HOW OUR LIVES TOGETHER
WILL FLORISH AND ENHANCE

I WILL FOREVER ENJOY YOU
NOTHING CAN CHANGE MY MIND
BECAUSE THE HAPPINESS GETS BETTER
TIME AFTER TIME

# HOLLA BACK

HOLLA BACK LADIES BECAUSE
YOU ARE THE BEST
YOU HAVE WHAT IT TAKES
AND NEVER MIND THE REST

ALWAYS STAND TALL AND
NEVER EVER FORGET
IF YOU GET THE FEELING
CALL ME QUICK, QUICK, QUICK

MAY GOD HOLD YOUR HEART
AS CLOSE AS HE CAN
MAY YOUR LIFE BECOME SIMPLE
OR JUST SO YOU CAN UNDERSTAND

AND WHEN SOME ONE THROWS A CURVE BALL
STEP BACK AND LET IT BE
FOR YOU HAVE FOUND
A FRIEND IN ME

# GOOD BYE

IT HURTS LIKE HELL
JUST SAYING GOOD BYE
IT HURTS LIKE HELL
FIGHTING NOT TO CRY

WHAT PART OF ME
HAVE YOU NOT TOUCHED
AND WHAT DO I DO
NOW THAT I LOVE YOU SO MUCH

JUST REMEMBER THAT DISTANCE IN LIFE LEAVES YOU
IN FEAR
BECAUSE THE ONE YOU TRULY LOVE
WILL SOON BE GONE, DISAPPEAR

IF NOT NOW THEN A LITTLE LATER
AND THAT'S WHEN THE DISTANCE
WILL BECOME SO POWERFUL
AND YOU'LL BECOME A HATER

# THIS HOUSE

DEAR LORD BLESS THIS HOME
BECAUSE FOR MANY DAYS
I HAVE BEEN ALL ALONE

WITH NO SPACE TO ADJUST
HAVING YOUR BLESSING
RIGHT NOW IS A MUST

I WILL NEVER UNDERSTAND WHY
WHEN THINGS LOOK IMPOSSIBLE
ALL I COULD DO IS CRY

BUT WITH A PRAY FROM YOU
MAKES ME BELIEVE THAT
LIFE CAN BE REALLY NEW

# BIOGRAPHY

I Was Born in New York City on the 5<sup>th</sup> day of August. I grew up in public schools and had the feeling that I was born to be a nurse. I began writing Poetry at the ripe age of nine. The thing that caught my heart in poetry was the Gut Catcher by E. E. Cummings.

Having a large family, all with different personalities gave me even more reason to write. I'm a mother of three daughters, and seven grandchildren. My goal is to write a series of poetry and greeting cards.